PAPER TRAIN

Echoes from Oxford

Poems by
Frederick Pheiffer

9/11/08

To Sue and Mike —
all good wishes!

[signature]

WingSpan Press

Printed in the United States of America

Published by WingSpan Press, Livermore, CA
www.wingspanpress.com

The WingSpan name, logo and colophon are the trademarks of
WingSpan Publishing.

ISBN 978-1-59594-218-0

First edition 2008

Library of Congress Control Number 2007940641

Other Books by Frederick Pheiffer

Furnace Brook Collected Poems

Badge No. 160 and other poems

The Last Stop

Acknowledgments

To my wife, Maryellen, her love, support and guidance encourages me to write. She gives me great solace.

Ed and Mary Ann McBride, good friends who have been with me from the beginning.

Special thanks to Tony Dempsey whose artistic energies helped me with my book.

Kate Dawidziak, the artist whose creative design graces the book's cover. Thanks Kate!

Dedicated to

Mike Dawidziak, Tony Dempscy
Corey & Dylan Hedderman
Ed McBride, Dick Reilly and Barry Weiss
- this cast of characters has made my life complete

Table of Contents

I. Paper Train

II. Pegasus

III. Echoes of Oxford

IV. Intercession

V. Marbleman

I

Paper Train

The best and most beautiful things in the world
cannot be seen or even touched – they must be felt with
the heart.

Helen Keller

Oxford Post Office

for Clint Lusk

Early morning gathering spot
for daily gossip and banter
people waited around for the mail
to be placed in their postbox.

Bea Hardiman was the postmistress
after her brother Tommy retired.
She knew everyone in town
a bit aloof, not wanting to be too friendly
didn't want people to think she was reading their mail.

Mike Haydusko also worked there
he always said hello,
and young Jimmy Lalley
started at the Oxford Post Office.

Many of Oxford's residents wanted their letters
delivered to a mail box in front of their homes.
Oxford's finest mail carrier was Clinton Lusk.
After leaving the Iron and Ore Mine
he carried the mail for many years,
never a bad word was said about him
he always did his job with a smile
and a kind word for everyone.

It has all changed.
Now there is a new post office across the street
no town buildings next to it, just a parking lot
people come and go
everyone is in a hurry these days
not much time for chitchat
many new folks have moved to Oxford
a lot of new faces with no ties to the past

and the old Oxford Post Office on Wall Street
is now a pizza parlor.

Old Oxford House Quoits

for Mary Alice Bockman

Kep's Old Oxford House
always had a crowd on Saturday night.
A bar and restaurant, doors opened early and
only closed when the last drinkers staggered out.

After a full week working in the mills
a couple of drinks and a game of quoits
eased the drudgery of the next work week.

Some patrons called quoits "indoor horseshoes,"
the players pitched the hard rubber discs
onto slate boards trying to get a ringer,
cold drinks in hand,
customers cheered as fierce competition carried over from week to week.

Rounds of drinks went to the winners.
Nick Hummer and Jimmy Secula could beat
most players.
Secula's ringers and leaners were legendary,
Hummer's skill in pitching close to the pin
won a lot of games.

On most Saturday nights in Oxford
these two never had to buy a drink.

All That's Left

The Oxwall factory water tower
looms over downtown
the old water tank is all that's left.

It seems to stand guard
over the piles of brick and debris
from the factory buildings.

For countless years
men and women worked at the Oxwall
laboring there all their lives
and now it is gone.

On moonlit evenings in Oxford
silent shadows move about
the factory's ruins
mournfully recalling
their years of toil.

Paper Train

During World War II
children's toys
were made of wood and paper.

One Christmas past
Santa Claus left
a toy paper train under the tree.

Julius the steam engine
pulling passenger and freight cars
with a red caboose.

Story boards were written on each car.
Lilly the Sleeping Car and Johnny the Dining Car
told their stories of life over the rails.
Box Car was unhappy until a hobo
came along for a ride.

With all the cars hooked together
they were pulled across the living room floor
endless hours of dreaming
as the young boy traveled by train
to far away places.

Through the passing of time
this paper train has never been forgotten
its whistle echoing over the years.

More Than Shuffle Board

After work and on weekends
Oxford's men played the game of shuffleboard
competing for shots & beers to quench their thirsts
after laboring in the ore mine and factories.

The Lackawanna House on Mechanic Street
had a long wooden shuffleboard table
against a wall in the barroom
players slid the weights to the end of the table
bumping the opponent off was key to victory.

A player like Joe Bernaski was legendary,
"Lefty" Haycock and Matt Naticzak
pushed a good weight as the men gathered
for friendly competition and drinks.

Going to Oxford's taverns and bars
was a way to relax and socialize
and catch up on the latest gossip.

Card games and darts were played
but nothing equaled the sound of one weight
knocking another off the table.

Miss Hankinson

Fourth grade teacher
at Oxford Central School.
She ruled her class
with an iron hand.
Strict order in her classroom
no talking or day dreaming.

She walked up and down the aisles
peering at students' work
looking for mistakes.
Homework done on time
or after school detention -
cleaning the erasers
by smacking them against the building
until the bricks were coated with white dust.

She relished teaching math
as pupils squirmed
trying to learn their long division.

When the school bell rang for dismissal
no one moved until she announced,
"now you may go."

After school hours
Miss Hankinson often played the piano.

Alone in her classroom
with her music
smiling to herself
gently touching the keys
soothing her soul.

Green's Sawmill

Del Green was a sturdy man
he operated the sawmill by himself.

Logs were delivered to the mill
pulled there by teams of horses.

A large circular saw cut the logs into lumber.
Sliding back and forth, on a moving platform,
each run of the jagged blade made new boards.

Piles of sawdust filled the yard
then taken away by the farmers
and used as bedding for their animals.

After a long day of work
Del Green would sit at the bar
in the Lackawanna House
cold beer in hand
negotiating for a fair price
for his lumber -

cut, stacked and readied by this solitary man.

First Day of Fishing

Furnace Brook was stocked with trout
from the hatchery for opening day.
Oxford's fishermen walked the banks
looking for their catch.

April 1 – the first day of fishing.
Leaving home early in the morning
with my rod and reel, a can of worms
and pieces of bread for bait.

Tossing the line into the water
a fish took the hook,
I reeled in my first catch ever,
on opening day.

Standing on the edge of Furnace Brook
hoping for more good luck
I remembered the refrain from my father –

" Fishy, fishy in the brook
daddy catch'em by the hook
mommy fry'em in a pan
baby eat them like a man."

Wall Street in Oxford

On one end of town - Ruther's Pharmacy.
Doc Ruther worked by himself
sometimes his wife Bessie helped.
He filled prescriptions with mortar & pestle
inside this cramped little store was a soda fountain
Doc's ice cream special was the banana split
hard to pass this one up
unless you didn't have the fifty cents to pay for it.

Across the state highway, Phil Kinney's Barber Shop
next to the Blacksmith Frank Koehn.
Many a cold winter night in Oxford
when men who drank too much
slept off the alcohol
warmed by the coals from the blacksmith's hearth.

Johnny Smith barbered in his shop by the highway
close to the Oxford House where shots of whiskey
and beers eased the drudgery after long work days.
Fichtel's sold hand packed containers of ice cream,
penny candies and comic books.

Louie Steinhardt's clothing and shoe store,
next door to Oram's Grocery store,
Kuhnsman's Hardware always had a large window
decorated for Christmas.

Townspeople shopped in Oxford stores
no malls or mega shopping centers back then
and if families didn't have the cash
names were written down in stores' books
until payment could be made.

Mountain Lake

The concrete pier still juts out into the water
but that's all that remains
of summer swimming at Mountain Lake.

At the end of the pier
children use to soar off the diving board
into the deep water
as others learned to swim
doing the doggy paddle.

The once sandy beach
now littered
with wind blown trash.

The outdoor roller rink closed
and Buckenmyer's Beach
at Mountain Lake
just a mournful memory.

Oxford's Saint Rose of Lima Church

The elevated altar where mass was celebrated
has been removed and taken away.

A new altar table at ground level
now the priest celebrates Mass
looking out at the congregation.

Pews removed from the back of the church
replaced by a bathroom
and "crying room" for ill-mannered children.

For such a long time, this little church
had given its faithful parishioners
comfort from life's hardships.

But ill winds had blown from Vatican II
taking away years of tradition
leaving faithful churchgoers
confused and lost.

Memorial Day Parade

for Rodney & Dorothy Wadhams

After WW II and the Korean War
America's small towns honored their veterans
with parades, speeches and moments of silence.

Belvidere, New Jersey, held a Memorial Day parade.
Marchers weaved through the streets of the town
crowds applauded as volunteer firemen passed by
with their red trucks polished to mirror perfection
onlookers laughed when they saw their reflections.

Folks cheered for the marching bands, veterans,
scout troops and Gold Star Mothers as they all passed by in splendid
formation.

The highlight of the parade - a hand made wooden boat
built by community volunteers.
It was placed atop a large wagon
and pulled along the parade route by the boy scouts.

Onlookers were always silent
some stood ramrod straight,
saluting as the boat passed by.

The parade ended at the bridge
spanning the Delaware River.
At the water's edge
bouquets of flowers
and small American flags
were placed on the boat
before it was gently pushed out from shore
into the river's swirling waters.

Bugler's "last taps" were sounded
as the small boat slowly drifted away.

Doctor Kimmel

for Bob & Nancy Friedman

Oxford had one doctor
his small office was part of the house
where he and his family lived.

Doc. Kimmel made house calls
with black bag in hand
and stethoscope dangling around his neck.

He popped a thermometer in the patient's mouth
admonishing his patient not to talk,
then voicing soothing words
he held a glistening needle in his hand.

After his bedside visit, he always had a moment to chat with the families
about their problems.

Going from house to house
in and out of his car
Doc. Kimmel treated Oxford's residents
with tender care.

Onion John

He lived in a one room cinder block dwelling
that he built on Dutch Hill in Oxford.

Onion John lived alone
he had no family.

He worked in Oxford and the surrounding area
doing yard work, gardening and odd jobs.

He didn't speak English
just nodded and smiled.

People paid him for his services
and gave him food to take home.

Onion John carried a gunnysack
walking from job to job
traveling by himself
wanting to be alone.

A solitary man
who somehow got by
until the day he died.

Circus Comes to Oxford

The big trucks drove into Oxford
parked and unloaded at Wilkinson's Field.

Hulking men labored with sledge hammers
and thick coils of rope
working to raise the big top
for the evening show.

The town's children raced to the field
to see the animals being unloaded and fed.

Opening night was a grand event
families dressed up for a special time out.

In the big tent, the ringmaster cracked his whip.
Trapeze artists swung on wires high above
acrobats tumbled about on the ground below
jugglers tossed colored balls into the air
and clowns played jokes on everyone.

Exotic dancers in flowing robes
a magician pulled a rabbit out of his hat
the "world's strongest man" lifted 2000 lbs.
high over his head and the "Tiger Woman"
snarled at everyone she saw
as the crowd roared with laughter.

Near the circus entrance
a barker called to one and all,
"step right up to see the egress
enter here for just five cents
a rare chance – once in a lifetime,

just a nickel to the egress!"

Company Store

In the town of Oxford Furnace
the Empire Steel & Iron Co. opened its store
in the early 1840's – selling groceries, dry goods
train tickets, farm items and in the basement
- a butcher shop.

The store was there until 1925.
After it closed, the Standard Silk Mill was there
followed by the Yankee Manufacturing Co.
and finally, the Oxwall Tool Company.

Hundreds of people worked in these factories
families from one generation to the next
labored at their jobs, trying to make a decent living.

Now the building is gone.
On the night of March 21, 2007 – the old building
was destroyed by a raging inferno
from deep in the basement to the slate roof
the fire consumed everything.

As the fire's smoke drifted into the night sky
souls of former workers
could be heard lamenting the loss.

Sadly, the townspeople had planned
to rehabilitate the building
returning it to its former glory
with small businesses.

All the plans and all the dreams
to make it a centerpiece for Oxford
disappeared in the smoke and fire

Never again
will the building's doors
be opened.

Card Game

for Mike Dawidziak

Most weeks in the homes of Oxford
dining room tables were stripped bare
extra chairs placed
for the Saturday night card games.

Work week over, neighbors got together
for a night out.

Radio music from the living room
cold drinks in the ice box
highballs are mixed
as the weekly card games begin.

A new deck of cards is opened
the dealer throws one card at a time
the players hands close to their chests
eyes dart about the table
looking for an opening bid
stakes are raised, bets called out
the pot increased, but some players fold.

All through the evening
there was more than a game of cards
as neighbors traded small talk
and the latest town gossip.

Canning

Summer and fall in Oxford
Ball jars were cleaned and readied
for canning of garden vegetables and fruits.

Bushel baskets of tomatoes were put up
for winter meals of mashed potatoes
smothered with stewed tomatoes.

Rows of jars with string beans,
peaches, pears and cherries filled
the pantry shelves.

Now the canning season is mostly lore
there's food from the freezer
or "fast food" – everything has changed
no need to have a garden
"too much work"
just stop at the supermarket
on the way home and get something quick,

and all those Ball jars
now used for holding loose change.

Steinhardt's Store

Louie Steinhardt sold galoshes, arctics
all sorts of overshoes and clothing
at his store in Oxford.

Employees from the mines and factories
all bought their boots from him.
Many spoke no English
immigrants from distant lands
Louie eased the workers fears
speaking with them in their native tongue.

Fathers brought their children to Steinhardt's
buying winter boots for walking to school –
no yellow buses back then.

Money was often scarce, wages were low
but Louie always said - "pay me when you can,
…I'll keep you on the book."

Stores like Steinhardt's are no more
just like the four buckle arctic boots
that the children use to wear.

Old Churches of Oxford

Danish Lutheran Church, German Reformed
First Presbyterian of Hazen, M. E. Church
St. Rose R.C. Church, Second Presbyterian
St. Nicholas Ukrainian Orthodox –
places of worship for Oxford's
long time residents and new immigrants.

Sunday services in native languages
offered some comfort to immigrant workers
many having left families behind.
Prayer books and hymnals in hand
voices sang out, giving praise to the Lord
for bringing them to America.

Monday to Saturday, Oxford's immigrants
toiled in the mills, mines, and factories
on Sunday, they dressed up for church.

Only a few of the old churches are left.

The German Reformed, Danish Lutheran
and the Ukrainian Churches are gone,
these sacred places of worship
just pictures on old postcards.

Insurance Man

Mr. Utter worked for Prudential Insurance
an insurance agent who sold policies
door to door.

He called on Oxford's families
selling insurance and collecting money,
the premium payments for most policies
cost twenty five cents a week.

At the end of the month
quarters were placed on the dining room table
for Mr. Utter to initial in his book - "paid."

He took time to visit with the housewives
chatting with them, catching up on town gossip
he never forgot a birthday or anniversary
he just seemed to fit in –
a part of the family.

Some people couldn't pay on time.
He would return days later
with an understanding demeanor
asked if they had the money -

somehow he would be paid.

II

Pegasus

Courage is being scared to death -
but saddling up anyway

John Wayne

Pegasus

for Dylan Hedderman

On a crisp autumn evening
my grandson and I sit on the front porch
waiting for the darkened sky to reveal
the Pegasus constellation.

Cream colored clouds cover the sunset
then lashes of red shoot through the cumulus
opening the mountain of clouds.

A golden horse flys through the chasm
coming directly at us
thundering hooves echo across the divide.

Its whinny beckons us
we climb onto the horde
holding its mane
our arms locked together
we fly off into the sky.

The sun is gone, evening begins.
Pegasus takes us into the heavens
the stars sparkle a welcome
a full moon warms us.

Riding this great steed
we are carried to places
we have never been.
Our hearts filled with laughter
never knowing such joy.

Thinking it was just a dream –
not so.
In my grandson's pocket
a packet of stardust
wrapped with hairs from a golden mane.

Together

for Maryellen

The hillside littered
with downed tree branches
from winter ice and snow.

It is now spring
grandmother and grandson gather the fallen boughs
building a burn pile
clearing the ground for the arrival
of the brilliant spring flowers
and soft green grass.

Without words between them
they work together.
Bending over picking up the brush
carrying arm loads to the enlarging pile.

She watches her grandson as he works
knowing within her heart
that he is a good person
and after she is gone
he will be more than capable
to carry on.

The Gift

After his grandfather died
he was bequeathed his books.
The youngster stares at the bookcase
so many old books covered with dust.

With no one else around
he pores over the books.

He opens "The Little House on the Prairie"
a story of a young girl and her family
moving out West to begin a new life
living in a log cabin, clearing the land
a family trying to survive.

Then a book about Uncle Wiggily Longears,
and his friend Nurse Jane Fuzzy Wuzzy,
life's unfolding adventures
through the eyes of the animals.

He sits in his grandfather's old chair
holding a book, recalling the times
when Pop-Pop had read to him.

Turning a page, he seems to hear a distant voice
speaking to him, telling the youngster
"the books will give you a lifetime of dreams."

Night Sounds

The stars hand suspended
never making a sound
the moon's shadow
moves silently through the woods.

From dusk to dawn
only stillness
from the sleeping
creatures of the forest.

Just an owl's wings
breaks the quiet
as it hunts through the dark.

Listening to the Radio

Before television, family entertainment
was the radio from morning to night.

Housewives began their day listening
to Rambling with Gambling on WOR,
then from Chicago – Don McNeil
and The Breakfast Club.

At night, the Green Hornet, Lone Ranger,
Fiber Magee & Molly, just some of the shows
that kept everyone glued to the radio.

Radio programs from far away.
Texaco's Saturday Opera from the Met,
Baseball from Brooklyn to the Bronx
as the Dodgers battled the Yankees
in the World Series and Notre Dame football
as listeners vicariously watched the game
in South Bend.

Old time radio captured the imaginations
of countless Americans,
enhancing their lives as they sat in front of the radio.

Little Cat

for Connie Moretti

I catch sight of your frail body
as you wander along the country road
searching for food.

Has someone abandoned you here?
Alone in this open space.

I hurry home to get
some food for you.

Returning with a filled bowl
I place it where I last saw you
hoping that you have seen me.

As I depart
I look back and see you
hunched over the food.

I know you will survive
until tomorrow
with food for comfort

and the prayers bring offered for you.

Horses

A hard frost blankets the meadow
sunrise glistens across the frozen grass.

As the horses enter the open field
they suddenly take off at a gallop
just because they want to.

Not because they have to.

Back and forth they go
racing each other
chasing the morning breezes
their hooves barely mark the frost.

Standing together
they glance around
waiting for her to see them
having so much fun.

Snorting to her
they voice their feelings
with a chorus of whinnies.

Away they gallop
running after the day's first shadows.

A Grand Day in County Clare

for Dick & Camille Reilly

The raging waves of the Atlantic
crash against the cliffs of Moher.

Never ending sounds from the ocean's roar.

High above the water's edge
a bagpiper's spirited music
celebrates Saint Patrick's day.

Leprechauns soon join in the morning song
tossing clusters of shamrocks into the air
raining good fortune everywhere.

Leaving the cliffs and fields of green
the path meanders past interlocking stone walls
we walk to the comfort of the cottage.

Resting by the fire
we give thanks for our blessings
on Saint Patrick's day.

A Young *Boy's Letter*

During WW II, the fourth graders
of Our Lady Of Lourdes School mailed a letter
to the captain of the USS Carroll, a navy destroyer.

In the envelope, a Miraculous Medal with the letter.
A young boy wrote, "Our class is praying for the ship and its crew
and for Sister Louise's brother
who serves with you. We think of you every day,
risking your lives so that we can go to school."

The captain was overcome with joy at this unexpected letter.
He put the Medal in a special place for the crew to see.

All the sailors visited this small shrine
offering prayers for their families and a special
thanks to the boy who wrote the words,
"God bless you for keeping us safe and free."

The USS Carroll shepherded convoys
across the Atlantic.
Unscathed from enemy attacks
the Carroll fought valiantly
all hands unharmed
no damage to the ship.

The captain wrote back to the students.
"We all believe your Miraculous Medal
has kept us safe in battle –
a wondrous shining light
as we fight tyranny."

Angels

for Tony & Virginia Mosca

Their wings beat against a celestial sky
as they gather the prayers
sent from below.

Opening the requests
reading them with pure delight
their work goes on throughout the night.

Collecting the prayerful messages
they fly off to see God
knowing that when He chooses
He can grant all things –

like make an angel
with golden wings.

Carl's Cigar

The work day began at 7am
men ran the lathes, grinders and cutting machines
shaping metal to make the valves.

Carl used calipers and ruler
setting the measurements on his lathe.

Man and machine
spinning the rough steel
routine work, day after day
boredom was ever present.

He toiled inside this lackluster factory
his work gave him a paycheck
providing for his family,
nothing more.

His one solace –
Carl would light up a cigar
while he worked,
and would gaze at his smoke rings
as they drifted off into space

Christmastime

for Peggy Stevens

As the snow dusts the ground
we carry our tree from the forest
leaving our tracks in the new fallen snow.

The tree's scent wafts through the house
lights are strung
treasured family ornaments
cover the Christmas tree.

The old Lionel train travels around the platform
its whistle echoing memories of Christmastimes past.

Candles are lighted in each window
a warming fire from the woodstove
the joyful music of Christmas carols
accompany the dogs' gentle snoring.

On top of the tree
a star shines its light
giving hope to all
on Christmas night.

Empty Shed

New snow covers the ground
drifts pushed against the shed's door
that once opened for the little pony.

She passed away on Valentine's Day
there is an eerier quiet here now.

The sun breaks through the clouds
shadows from the fence
grace the fresh snows
like angels lined up in prayer.

Standing here – I recall all those days
when the pony's whinny greeted me.

I sensed then that we were connected
and I would always hear her calling to me.

Today as I mourn her death
the sound of her voice
fills the sky around me.

Connemara Ireland

The thatched cottage at water's edge
beckons me to rest
blue silk waters touch the shore
far off mountains tower against a cloudless sky
stone fences mark this patch of earth.

A pony knickers
to the sound of my footsteps
I've returned to my ancestor's home.

Opening a weathered door
a room with bricks of peat
stacked next to the hearth.
My grandmother's empty tea cup on the table.

Lighting the peat
the fire's warmth
brings back her stories
memories of our moments together.

Calling His Dogs

An old man walks from his home
across the fields into the woods
looking for his dogs
that have run off.

Whistling for them to come back
he continues with heavy heart
calling out their names
hoping they're not harmed.

Wondering how they got out
he mutters to himself,
"must have left the door open."

Calling again and again as he crosses a stream
he slips and falls into the water
unable to free himself
he cries out.

Racing over the fields from the woods
his dogs come to him
they crawl under his arms
and help him up.

Together, they leave the water's edge
and head for home,
giving comfort to each other.

Penny the Pony

A few years ago, I met Penny while walking
a country road near my home.
Picked her some clover and dandelion greens
and introduced myself.

Next day, I did the same.
A daily ritual thus began
we soon became friends.

Each visit I called to her,
"how is the little girl"
she always answered with a loud nicker
trotting to greet me
she looked for a treat.

She soon gave me her affection
and all I did was give her some attention and love.

We often stood together in the morning sun
I'd brush her coat
as she rubbed her head against me

Tonight's phone call brought sad news
Penny had died today
I can't believe she is gone.

I'll continue my walks by her place
and visit were we met
I will ask God to bless her
and to keep her safe.

III

Echoes from Oxford

To be yourself in a world that is constantly trying
to make you something else
is the greatest accomplishment

Ralph Waldo Emerson

Oxford's First Fire Truck

The Oxford Volunteer Fire Department
established in 1946
the townspeople now had hope.
In the past, Belvidere or Washington fire companies
responded from miles away to fight Oxford's fires.

On a crisp January day
Fire Chief Johnny Esposito
drove a brand new 1947 International Fire Truck
into town – what a grand event!

The truck was parked in front of the new firehouse
built by local folks and the firemen.

On dedication day, the townspeople gathered
at the firehouse to admire their bright red truck.
The Ladies Auxiliary made homemade pies & cakes.

Quite a triumph back then
for this small town
somehow getting its very own fire truck
they showed the big towns that it could be done!

Quarries of Oxford

Limestone was taken from Oxford
in the late 1800's to the 1940's.
the sandy sedimentary rock
was carried by train to New Village
where it was made into cement.

Years after, the quarries were worked for stone
then crushed for highways
massive boulders were removed
and taken to the Jersey shore for jetties.

Later – the abandoned quarries filled with water
ignoring the "no trespass" signs
youngsters snuck into the quarries
for swimming and daredevil diving
from the high rock ledges.

Taunting each other to climb to the highest spot
a fearless few dove from fifty feet up
graceful flights into the deep blue waters.

Others scaled the rock to lesser heights
no sandy beaches here
this was all about how high you could climb
and once up there, having the courage to dive.

School Street Cisterns

Between School Street and Bull Run
arching concrete shelters covered
endless running spring waters.

Long before wells and town water
families drew their daily water with buckets
for drinking, cooking and washing.

Children played at the cisterns
games of hide & seek in the tall grasses
perfect places to stay hidden
until racing to the base
and calling out "safe."

After the games, everyone hung out there
dipping glasses into the clear waters
thirsts nicely quenched
until it was time to go home.

Selling Door to Door

First it was Phil Voseler
going through town
with his horse and wagon
selling his garden fresh vegetables
and homegrown strawberries.

Next was Willie Bush with his truck
driving all over town
selling fruits, vegetables and groceries.

Stopping in front of Oxford's houses
honking his truck's horn
he had awnings on the side of the truck
for shade as he sold to the housewives.

Willie was always good for the latest gossip
and if a family was a bit short for cash
he would nod his head
put what was owed in his book
knowing he'd be paid next time.

Gumballs

A penny was put into the slot
of the gumball machine,
with a hard turn of the handle
the gum dropped into the chute.

Fichtel's store had the gumball machine.
It held solid colored balls
red, green, blue and orange
but it was the striped ball that everyone wanted.

Playing for the prized gumball
was an after school delight
small time gambling in Oxford –
all for a penny,
imagine that!

Oxford's Junkmen

They called out in booming voices,
"we want your rags, bottles, clothes
and scrap iron – all the stuff you don't want
we'll take it for free."

Bob Heater the junkman from Dutch Hill
was aggressive as he worked the streets
never missing a chance to take something away.

His truck was always piled high with rags
and odds and ends
stuff that only he wanted.

With a rasping voice after a day's work
he could be found in one of Oxford's taverns
having a drink or two
while trying to sell his wares
to anyone who would listen.

Oxford Central School Song

"Oh Oxford School to you we sing
the best in sportsmanship will bring
to do our best in every way
in all our work and all our play...."

Students sang the school song when gathered
in the auditorium for the weekly events.

After the show, teachers led the students back to their classrooms,
hoping to inspire them with their erudition, but it's the names of some
of the teachers that are remembered -Mr. Wolf-music teacher, always
hunting for the right notes.
Mrs. Slack-taught math, never slow in checking every students homework.
Mr. Fox-school janitor, quick as a fox in his work.
Mr. Fisher-school principal, like the mammal,
he would catch you cutting classes.
Miss Riddle- no mystery here, just a great kindergarten teacher,
quite an array of names with matching personalities.

"Oh Oxford School, hurrah for the blue & gold
we'll try to do our best for you
and keep our courage true...."

Pea Shooter

It's the end of June and school's out in Oxford
the boys roam the woods
looking for wild cherry trees
with hard green cherries for their shooters
ready to have fun.

Each boy picks handfuls
placing them in their pockets
they hurry back to town.

With shooters in hand
they hang out by Fichtel's store
firing away at unsuspecting people
with each hit
the boys would run and hide
laughing at what they had done.

Tinkers, Gypsies and Hobos

Oxford had them all visit
some stayed but most kept going on
from town to town.

The Tinkers with wagons and horses
camped outside of town
repairing pots and pans
working odd jobs
it was their way of life.

Hobos rode the DL&W railroad trains
from Scranton to Hoboken and back,
Oxford was a half-way place to camp
communal cooking and sleeping near the tracks
a world that Hobos shared
until they caught the next train out.

Gypsies visited Oxford offering fortune telling
they worked the bars regaling the locals
with stories from their world adventures.

Saturday Night Bath

Large pots of water were heated on a coal stove
carried upstairs from the basement
and poured into the tub
to heat the tepid water.

Every Saturday night, a ritual
Oxford's children sat in tubs
weekly wash up for Sunday church.

After the bath
a bowl of popcorn
then off to bed.

Homemade Fudge

Coal fired kitchen stove
cast iron frying pan
mixture of sugar, butter
chocolate and walnuts.

We gathered around the stove
watching the fudge fill the pan
as the winter snows swirled outside.

A Saturday night treat
sitting in front of the radio
listening to a show
as we savored mom's homemade fudge.

Tricycle

Three wheels and wooden blocks
taped to the pedals
the boys legs barely touching the pedals
as his father pushed
while leaning over him.

His dad gently shoved him down the street
he pedaled as fast as he could go
flying along like the wind
riding his tricycle
to places he had never been.

Coal Bins

Homes in Oxford were heated
by coal fired furnaces in the basements.

Dump trucks brought the anthracite coal.
Backing up to cellar windows or doors
the long steel chutes were hooked together
as the dump lifted up high
the coal slid down the chute
into the coal bins.

A half ton was usually ordered
sometimes less –
it all depended on the price
and how much money
there was for the coal.

Baseball in Oxford

for Bev & Charlie Brewer

Oxford's baseball team was feared by all
opposing teams couldn't hit the ball
Oxford's pitchers threw mighty strikes
as umpires called, "you're out" with delight.

Swish of the bat was heard far and wide
as Oxford played with skill and pride.

"Oxford's boys" as they were called
had a knack for the game of baseball.

Talent and character
a desire to win
the boys tore through the Tri-County league
defeating their opponents, again & again.

Names like Cryan, Hummer, Secula
Bockman, Jones and Delaney- legends
from a time long gone.

The sound of the umpires voice
still echoes off Oxford's hills -
"Batter up- let's play ball."

Scouting

for Bill Cryan

Scouts from Oxford's Troop 111 hiked
high mountain terrain
to the Delaware Water Gap
then to Sunfish Pond
after day long trailblazing in the Appalachians
they head back to camp
a fire is lighted for the evening meal.

Day is done
scouting skills were tested
merit badges awarded after supper.

Pup tents readied for the night
the weary boys soon slumbered off.

Camping along the Delaware
friendships formed
lifetime of memories
never to be undone.

Swing

Thick sturdy ropes
tied to the biggest limb
of the old cherry tree,
a board for the seat.

A father pushes the swing
with ever gentle touch
propelling his son up into the sky
back and forth
legs kicking out
higher and higher
the swing goes,

with only the sound of laughter
breaking the silence
between father and son.

The Old Outhouse

One and two seated outhouses
on patches of ground
behind Oxford's homes.

A flashlight or lantern lighted the small shed
empty coffee can covered the toilet paper
often bees and wasps made their homes there.

A mad dash from house
to outhouse
braving all kinds of weather
no heated seats against the winter cold
rugged days back then.

Only a few families had a three holed outhouse
very special status
imagine what was said
when three people sat together.

Greyhound Post House

Bus travel in the 1940's and 50's
from New York City to the Poconos
and all points west
was a long and tiresome trip
with two lane highways
speed limits strictly enforced
travel seemed to take forever as buses stopped
for passengers at all the towns along the way.

Halfway between NYC and the Pennsylvania mountains
was the Greyhound Post House
in Bridgeville, New Jersey.

Royal Blue Coach, Great Eastern Bus
and Greyhound all stopped at the Post House.
Travelers disembarked for a rest stop
thirsty and hungry, meals were served all hours
the riders devoured their cafeteria food.

Passengers could buy bags of candy, gum and
sunglasses before getting back on the bus
for the rest of their journey.

The Post House was demolished years ago
now, just a vacant spot of land along the highway
with no sign or marker to tell the story
about the countless people who traveled by bus
before airplanes took over!

Oxford General Store

Entering the store in downtown Oxford
warm greetings from the Stires family
hot coffee, breakfast sandwiches
lottery tickets and newspapers to start the day.

Fichtel's Store was here first.
Ice cream & soda fountain
comics, magazines and penny candies.
A phone booth at the rear of the store
not many folks had phones then.

After ma and Vic Fichtel passed away
only Mulligan worked at keeping the old store
as it was in the beginning.

Over the years – townspeople wondered if
"it will ever be the same again."

Today, the old place feels the same.
New patrons are greeted warmly
old customers are coming back
Tastycakes & pics are still on the shelves
and the small town gossip
doesn't get any better.

IV

Intercession

Denial ain't just a river in Egypt

Mark Twain

Serenity

for Keir Aspin

Breaking a trail through the new snow
skis pushing the white powder aside
long gliding strides
through the quiet woods.

Small birds fly from the pine trees
looking for early morning seed.
A hawk circles the sun
staying in its light
searching for nourishment

Fields of unbroken snow
before me
making new tracks.

Not looking back
I push on.

After the Funeral

When all the prayers were spoken
and flowers put on the grave
my father moved off from everyone
to be alone.
Trying to find his final words
to his wife
not wanting to say good-bye.

I heard him speak to her
"the earth has hold of you now
all your suffering is over
and when my time comes
I will fly on a cloud to meet you
and we will finally be together again."

Holding my father's hand
we turned away from the grave
got into the car
and drove home
together.

A Veteran Remembers

At the nursing home on Monday mornings
residents gather to talk and reminisce
recalling events from many years ago.

Charles Spellman spoke today
about his Navy service in WW II.
He served aboard the USS Ingersoll
a destroyer commissioned in 1943.

He was a "plank holder"
the nickname for the first crew.

He talked about the war
fighting in the Pacific
encountering the enemy
meeting their attacks
with guns blazing from his ship.

In the heat of battle
his shipmates stuck together they never wavered
duty bound
they fought with valor.

The record shows he served with honor
Charles Spellman is proud to be a veteran
and to have his war service memorialized.

He fought for his country
when asked if he would serve again,
he simply replies –

"It would be an honor."

Alone on the Farm

She sits alone at the kitchen table
the funeral is over
everyone is gone.

Endless years of work together
keeping the farm going
animals always fed
and now,
for the first time
she is alone.

She listens for his voice
hoping to hear him say,
"chores are all done,
let's go sit on the couch."

There are no sounds
only unfamiliar shadows
that she will see
for the rest of her life.

Warren Haven

Warren Haven is the final home
for people who are ill or infirmed
and need special attention.

Some of the residents have no one left
while others have family who visit
and some relatives simply don't care.

A few occupants call out for loved ones
other residents just sit for hours
some stay in bed wanting to be left alone.

Warren Haven's staff works hard
to make each person's life
a little better,

for these caregivers
it's not always easy.

A Father's Distress

Sitting alone
in the back yard of his home
a father softly cries
his daughter has not stopped drinking.

He just found another empty bottle
hidden in the pantry
behind the groceries.

Time after time
she assured him,
"I've stopped drinking -
I'll never have another drop of alcohol,"
only to repeat the lie
again and again.

Just sitting there
bathed in tears
he was never the same.

His Eyes and Heart

The dog was discarded after living
with someone for twelve years.
Put in a shelter to be forgotten.

He captivated her
the moment she saw him
she adopted this Springer Spaniel
and named him "Squiggle T. Britches."

He greeted her each day with wiggles
and a smile unending,
but what captured her heart was his eyes
glowing with love, wanting her to see him.

Squiggles gave love from a heart
as big as a full moon
all he ever wanted
was her love and devotion in return.

And now he is gone.
The cancer got to him.
He fought so hard to survive
his only purpose in life
was to give!

Nursing Home Solitude

Residents sit in front of the television
staring into space with blank faces
numb to everything around them
another uneventful day.

Waiting out their loneliness
resembling leaves on the trees
hoping for a gentle summer sun
before the autumn comes
sending them to rest.

Intercession

Early morning walk into the woods
I think of you.

Tree branches empty
frost colored leaves
lay upon the ground.

My prayer lifts away
catching a gentle breeze
as snow begins to fall.

Each day begins and ends
with hope filled words
asking God
to help you in the days to come.

Gathering

Nursing home residents gather
each morning to hear
the local newspaper being read.

News and headlines read first
then the horoscopes, obits and sports
the listeners sit quietly in their wheelchairs
visualizing the comics
and hearing Ann Lander's advice
to the lovelorn.

The obituaries are read and talked about –
"I remember him, a good guy,"
"she was a heck of a gal,"
"knew her family,"
the comments adding a final note
to the daily death notices.

Soon some of the residents doze off
others gaze longingly out the windows
dreaming of days gone by
wondering why they are here
trying not to think about the day
when their obits will be read and someone else
will be listening from a wheelchair.

Nancy Molomo

It's her smile
and her eyes
they sparkle.

Holding hands
we share stories
about growing up
in small town of Oxford.

We talk about her mother
she was special
always had a kind word for everyone.

Visiting with Nancy at Warren Haven
memories and stories shared
the room fills with our laughter.

When it's time for me to go
she asks, "Will you be coming back?"

With a nod of my head,
I murmur – "yes."

Memories of Mary Cantoni

Oh how everyone enjoyed Mary's company
the other residents and staff looked forward
to Mary's daily "words of wisdom,"
she always had their attention.

Mary lived at Pleasant Valley Infirmary –
a county nursing home.
Her humor was unending!

Mary regaled in English & Italian
we could usually understand her
because her hands moved when she talked.

She prayed daily to St. Francis of Assisi,
but only in Italian,
asking him to answer her petitions,
especially winning at Bingo.

She was everybody's mother
gave advice whether you wanted it or not
and opened her heart to all.

V

Marbleman

Is often said there is nothing better for the inside
of a man than the outside of a horse

Ronald Reagan

Hall of Fame

for Ed McBride

The umpire calls "batter up,"
scored tied, bottom of the ninth inning
"Tuts" McBride steps to the plate
takes the first pitch for a called strike
next ball is fired at the batter – dusting him off.

Stepping out of the batter's box
he stares at the pitcher
no words are spoken.

Moving to the plate, he patiently waits
a blazing fastball comes in waist high
with one mighty swing
the ball flies off the bat and over the fence
bases are cleared, a grand slam wins the game
for Colgate University.

After the cheering and congratulations
McBride walks back onto the field
reliving the moment
the sound of the bat still reverberating
across the Chenango Valley
all the way to the streets of Utica
where McBride learned the game.

Reflecting on his determination to succeed
he gives thanks for all his blessings
from classroom to the field

a long way from the hardships
of his immigrant ancestors.

Morning Clouds

for Corey & Susan

On this autumn morning
fog covers the valley
blanketing the drumlins.

Milking done, the farmer opens the gate to a field
his cows plod silently from the barn
soon lost in the heavy mist.

Holding onto the family farm
he works alone
his life filled with endless chores.

Each day begins and ends the same
long hours of hard work
trying to make ends meet
as the bills pile up on the kitchen table.

The sun finally cuts through the mist
driving his tractor to cut the hay
he says a prayer
asking for help
to get him through the day.

Old Cherry Tree

for Connie Gavin

Outstretched branches filled with summer fruit
ladders placed against the tree
buckets carried up to collect the cherries
then taken into the house
pitted and put into steaming pots
for canning and jelly.

Jars of cherries line the pantry shelf
for autumn pies.

Thick slabs of homemade bread
smothered with peanut butter
and cherry jelly
a mouth watering treat
anytime of the year.

Departing Souls

A cloud filled with angels
sails through the heavens.
They look down at earth
searching for souls departed
to take them to places that God has decided.

One soul hovers in space.

With wings unfolding
an angel flies to her side
with helping hands
wiping away the tears
giving comfort by saying,
"Don't worry, Heaven is near."

Words tumble out from this despondent soul
"In my last days on earth I had this fear
that God wouldn't know me
and I would hang helplessly alone
in this eternal sky."

Not to be was the quick reply,
you are to go with us
God wants you forever
at his side.

This Heart

My love and devotion to you
has given me a peace that I thought
I would never have.

You have given me a life
filled with song.
You have held me in your arms
when the dark tries to take over my soul.

You have opened your heart
and given me your love
it means so much to me that you are my wife
and the only one I will ever love.

Steve's Hot Dog Stand

Steve sold hot dogs and sodas in the 1950's.
Steamed rolls, mustard and pickle on the dog
gruff words were free with every sale.

He worked inside his tiny stand
stuck to the side of a brick building
in Washington, New Jersey.

Buses stopped there
before traveling to Oxford, Buttzville,
and towns along the Delaware River.
Passengers bought "two to go," for their trip home.

High school football players yelled to Steve
from their school buses –"free hot dogs if we win."
He always answered back, "nothing in life is free,
especially from me."

Steve's hot dogs are a thing of the past
along with the small stand
but his sharp wit and wily words
remain on the pages of memory.

A Musical Pun

My heart was baroque
when my bow left me.

She had strung me along
fine tuning my life.

Pitching me aside
as she crossed a new bridge.

Washington Movies

for Tony Dempsey

High school date at the movies
box of popcorn and soda.

Strolling into the theater, hand in hand
looking for back row seats in the balcony
with no one else nearby.

We watch the news clips,
followed by the bouncing ball
everybody sings along,
"take me out to the ball game,
buy me some peanuts & crackerjacks,
I don't care if we ever get back...."

The lights go out
the movie house is dark.
I put my arm around her
without a murmur
she snuggles close to me,

as the screen lights up
to the sound of my beating heart.

We Are Blessed

Each horse and dog at Last Stop
depends on us for their care.

After evening feeding
one of the horses rubs his head
across my wife's back
showing affection.

Throaty noises from the dogs
tails ever wagging
time for evening treats.

Every day, the animals show their gratitude
all they want is for us to love them in return.

For Whom the Bell Tolls

The casket is lowered into the ground
a bell resonates across the Alleghenies.

The bell tower's shadow
casts a quiet onto the snow
Brother Marion has died.

He had pulled the bell's rope
calling the friars to daily prayers.

As they walked through the pines to chapel
their footsteps harmonized
with the clarion call of the bell.

Dirt is shoveled on the casket
the bell is silent, only the sound of the friars' voices
can be heard, as they praise their lost Brother.

Winter winds soon lift the swirling snow
covering the bell tower,
in the grey daylight
a veiled apparition appears
grasping the rope one last time.

For the Students at Southgate School

Opening my book of poems
I read to the students about the animals
that live with us at Last Stop.

Rescued horses and dogs are given a fresh start.
Freedom to run and play
now safe from past fears.

The students listen as I paint word pictures
of the animals' new lives
the magic in the air
with the animals knowing
this is their last stop.

Prayer for an Animal

The cottontail rabbit sits hunched
alone in the tall grass
listening to sounds from the forest
dew blankets the pasture
evening has come.

The animal sees me
it doesn't run.

I stand still sensing its loneliness
a need for this creature
to sit there with me.

I ask an angel to shield this creature
when it roams through the night.

The Neighbor

When he drank
he was out of control.
When he was sober
not a finer person around.

The nights were the worst
staggering home from the bars of Oxford
he heaped abuse upon his wife and children
unable to stop his drinking
he blamed everybody but himself.

After each binge
he worked in suit and tie
hiding his addiction.

During times of sobriety
a promise was made to everyone
this was the "last time"
and just as quick – it came undone.

The years passed, his children left him
his wife lived on in despair
never able to leave him.

When his life ended
he was found lying on the ground
with an empty bottle in his hand.

Watching Lawrence Welk

for Scott Donnini & family

Black & White television
and Lawrence Welk's Orchestra
playing their "champagne music"
on Saturday nights
in living rooms across America.

Easy listening music
toe tapping tunes
pleased audiences week after week
especially in New Village, New Jersey.

Lou Donnini's mother cooked supper early
then we all sat in front of the TV
to watch Lawrence Welk
it was her Saturday night out.

With his trademark smile and broken English
Welk had her total attention.
English was a difficult language for Senora Donnini
it was the music she understood, not his words.

Two young guys in the 1950's
just wanting to go out for the night
had to sit and watch the show
because Mrs. Donnini said so.

Gary Scranton

for Debbie Scranton

His soul moves in the morning light
traveling amongst the clouds
warmed by the sun.

His spirit wanders across the valley
flying over where he once lived
moving with soft breezes
he silently rests next to you.

Each evening, a star guides his soul
to the gentle warmth of the moon.

When you pray for him
you will hear him singing
his voice echoing off the beyond,
"the suffering has ended –
my soul is free."

Marbleman

Father and son worked the quarries
cutting the marble stone from the mountain.

Marble men
dust filled their lungs
chiseled hands held tools of their work.

Working on his new book
the son looks at his stone carver's hands
marked lines cut across his palms
holding images of his father.

Putting down his writing
he moves across the room
stares out the window
the moon's light rests softly on his face.

A shadow glides by holding tablets of stone
the spirit calls out, "I can hear the words you write,
echoing off the quarry walls."

With unlimited joy
Marbleman steps outside into the night
reaching up
he touches his father's hand.

Father Vincent Negherbon

With his infamous scowl
Father Vincent patrolled
the college campus and Raymond Hall
eager to catch the students
who were breaking his laws.

He did eventually calm down
became Dean and College President
brought a lot of class
to this small Pennsylvania town.

When we reflect on his service
to Saint Francis College
we will remember him in the library
with an open book and a smile on his face
thanking God for giving him at last
the honor to be the Librarian
of this most wonderful place.

Poems

Students gather in the classroom
lunchtime poetry readings
by these young children
courageous efforts in front of their peers.

One child reads from her notebook
the words paint a picture of sadness
her father never visits
he has never come back.

His shadow fills her words
tears put into verse
from a child's broken heart.

March 17th

for Bev & Ned Russell

On the fields of Shannon green
Leprechauns dance unseen
holding garlands of shamrocks high
their laughter fills the clear blue sky.

Spring flowers open to the morning sun
creatures of the forest join in the fun.

A lark's song revels in the meadow morn
for on this blessed day, Saint Patrick was born.

Ron Collins

He grew up in Oxford
Cat Swamp is where he lives
retired school teacher
and now a volunteer.

Ron Collins visits with the residents
at the county nursing home.

A caring and warm person
he shows up, arms filled
with magazines, newspapers and books
he makes himself right at home.

Ron kids with the residents
making small talk
allaying their fears with comforting words.

Understanding their loneliness
he brightens their days
with good cheer.

He always asks each person,
"How are you today,"

and with this simple question
he opens closed hearts
for at least
another day.

Valentine I

From morning sun
to evening hours
I think of you

when the stars fill the night sky
I think of you

and every moment of my life
I will be with you.

Epilogue

The Town of Oxford, New Jersey still is a magical place in my life. I grew up there and all my experiences as a boy are recorded in my memory. These events come back to me each time I write, and some are in this book as poems.

To all the grand people of Oxford – you will never be forgotten!

Printed in the United States
201678BV00007B/31-54/A